DIFFERENT WORLD,
SAME PLANET

DIFFERENT WORLD, SAME PLANET

The call of life

JOSEPH M. DACCACHE

authorHOUSE®

AuthorHouse™ LLC
1663 Liberty Drive
Bloomington, IN 47403
www.authorhouse.com
Phone: 1-800-839-8640

Published by AuthorHouse   02/04/2014

ISBN: 978-1-4918-6124-0 (sc)
ISBN: 978-1-4918-6112-7 (hc)
ISBN: 978-1-4918-6163-9 (e)

Library of Congress Control Number: 2014902410

"The life of the individual has meaning insofar as it aids in making the life of every living thing nobler and more beautiful."

—Albert Einstein

I dedicate this book to my friends, family, and every person I met in the journey of my life. Some of you walked with me for a mile while others for a few thousand miles. Each of you has made my life nobler and more beautiful in your own way. I will never forget your influence on my life and I will always remember the good times that we had together.

A Special Thank You

To my dad and mom for their love and the value they put in my heart. To my wife Katia, my best friend, for her unconditional love and support. To my children, Chris and Jenny, for being always a source of joy and pride.

This book would never have become a reality without the hard work, the talent, and the patience of my great friend and editor, Marko. Thanks to him I found the courage to start and finish this book and so many other books.

And thank you my dear Jenny for spending so many nights helping me find the right words and correcting my spelling.

Preface

This story is a true story. This is my life. Life happens like an earthquake that you never expected or saw coming. It hits you and you react. You deal with the consequences. Either it breaks you or it builds you. It can destroy you or make you wiser. It's all about what you choose to make out of it.

Life is so unique, it happens once and we do our best to protect it. We're not angels even if sometimes we like to think that we are, nor are we demons, even if sometime we behave like one. We are human and therefore we have the amazing capability to be both, angels and demons, we switch back and forth between the two.

We make decisions and have the possibility to change our mind at any time. We can be heroes or we can be evil. Even if we enjoy the light, every so often we settle to live in the dark. Sometimes instead of choosing right versus wrong; we choose survival.

My life is a story of big dreams; dreams that came true, of great hopes and deceptions, fears, exile, and broken promises. It's a story of choices and consequences. Most of all, it is a story of an unconditional love, a continual struggle, and a battle to protect life. The earthquake that hit me was so devastating that everyone, even myself, was convinced that It would kill me. And yet, here I am. I hold on to all of the love I have and the promises I made.

I survived.

I am alive.

I can make choices.

I can make a difference.

I will.

Introduction

Today, I find myself sitting at my desk looking at a picture of Charley on the wall. In the picture he is four months old. He clings to me as I have my arms wrapped around him in a protective embrace.

It seems like a lifetime ago, but it's only been six years since my life took a huge turn. I am tempted to say that my life lost its meaning but that is not true. The clothing of a victim has never fit me.

I was born and lived in a country of war, blood, and death. A country that so many poets named as the land of milk and honey but our reality was very different. We were a society that was always at war. We were killing each other constantly and the reasons for the killing changed rapidly. It was always something "different" and yet, somehow the same. The sound of bombs and the rhythm of war was the record playing in the background of my childhood.

I lived in a world where everything was expensive, but life was cheap. A brother would kill his brother for ideals that changed depending on the interests of the princes of wars and the leaders of the factions.

I don't want to keep talking about this, instead, I would rather talk about the meaning behind this book. It's been six years since the urge of writing my story began and continued to burn strong. But, I never took the first step to embark in this adventure. Every time I considered laying the foundation, my mind created a thousand excuses to neglect it.

First of all, I am not a writer nor am I a philosopher. I don't have revolutionary ideas and I don't want to change the world. I have always been a man of action and a big dreamer not someone who would sit still and write. The dreams I had were not common in the land where I grew up.

I have always guided my life towards my dreams and saw the accomplishment of them coming forth each day. Every time I introduced my dreams and my projects, the word 'impossible' seemed to be the monotonous and repetitive towards my aspirations.

With time, the impossible that my surroundings threw at me became the fuel of my motivation. Over the years the most ardent proclaimers of the impossible became my strongest believers. I was a warrior of life fighting to create a dream in a country of death. A country ripped apart by the hate and suffering of its people. I wanted to defend life. Life in all of its forms.

Waiting was never my best or strongest habit. When I wanted to accomplish something I did everything to put life into it and even the cosmos became my compass. But, I believe that I was only able to do so because I knew what I longed for and was willing to pay any price. For six years, I've been uncertain of what I am searching for. Now I know.

I know that I want my life back.

In one of my attempts to find a job, I met Marko. Immediately a kind of understanding and friendship developed. After leaving the company, the friendship remained and continued to prosper. We kept meeting on a regular basis and talking about the past and the future.

Between these conversations Marko said that the story I lived was worth being told. One day, while conversing, he opened his laptop and started typing every word that I said. That moment was the spark of ignition that I needed to start a new journey. We began the telling of my story.

I'll let each one of you decide the meaning behind the book.

My Early Years

My school years were punctuated by many periods of intense war. Just getting to school was dangerous and not guaranteed. A school bus used to take us there and on the way to school we had to go through multiple militia checkpoints of the different factions at war. Many times the driver asked all of us students to cover our heads and duck down to protect ourselves because there were snipers. Each time the fear in the bus was palpable but this was our existence.

My day-to-day life was an adventure of survival and a mixture of fears and hopes. It wasn't until later in age that I understood why my mom would say goodbye to me every morning in such an emotional way. In time, through perseverance, a little luck, and determination I received a B.A. in Special Education from St. Joseph University in Beirut.

The only way to keep going in such conditions was to have hope to keep the constant fear at bay. Hope comes from dreams. I always refused in my mind to accept what everybody kept repeating to me: that this is what life is. Life is not just survival or the simple lack of death. There is something more to it. At that time I didn't know what more was but I didn't want to accept the fact that life has no value.

I remember that, as a child, when I was about eight years old I didn't have any good grades. I would like to say that my dreadful grades were caused by the war and not because I was lazy. In reality, I preferred to read super hero stories instead of my school textbooks. I would even hide a comic inside the pages of the book while pretending to do my homework.

My dad used to threaten me by telling me that if I didn't improve my grades the only thing he would be left to do was to buy me a herd of sheep and I would become their shepherd. Unfortunately for him, this idea appealed to me instead of frightening me and made me dream of my flock. In my dreams I would travel around being free with the flock. Whenever it was a stressful period with bombs going off, I would close my eyes and imagine being with my sheep in a peaceful pasture.

When all my friends used to draw pictures of wars and destruction, inspired by my flock, I would draw animals and farms. I could draw my farm in great detail. In time though, the dream faded as the reality of survival imposed itself.

Then, in University, I met someone who shared my love of life and animals. Katia, who is now my wife, had always adopted stray animals and helped them to live in peace. She shared her sanctuary with me. My dream was reignited and found its way back into my life. When I graduated from University this dream kept calling to me.

Upon graduation we followed the regular career paths of new graduates. We worked in our fields of expertise. Katia was a teacher at a regular school and I worked with people with disabilities. We lived in an apartment and the only animals we had were a pair a hamsters. In our free time we would go and visit farms and build friendships with other people who had the same passion for life.

At the place where I worked with my students with disabilities; **there was some spare land**. I used this land to host some animals to help with our therapy. Over time, this collection of animals became larger and more varied and we began to call it the farm.

After six years of waking up every day hoping that something would change, looking at the picture of Charley and wondering what's next, I began to write my story. It all started in 1995. Only a year after my beautiful daughter, Jenny, was born.

Charley

All the animals in the farm were received from hunters or the government because they were illegal to traffic. But even if it was illegal it was not considered a serious crime. The police did not prosecute the traffic of illegal animals. Animals of all kinds were sold on the street. Even if we had tried to save all the animals by buying them off of the streets we would have been unable to do so since there were so many. Plus, we would also be feeding the traffickers and we didn't want that.

When we encountered a trafficker or a seller we wouldn't buy from them no matter what the conditions were. We would just try to talk some sense into them.

Once, when we were on one of the main roads, we saw someone with a small cage. In that cage was something I had never seen before, a baby chimpanzee. And after an hour of trying to convince the seller how cruel it was to do what he was doing. we ended up paying the money because we knew that if left in the cage for another day the chimpanzee would die.

The chimpanzee was so young and in bad shape. He was about one month old or maybe even less. We knew that to catch a baby chimpanzee in the wild the traffickers had to kill a bunch of adult chimpanzees to be able to steal him from his mother. The baby was really sick. I gave him the name Charley. Giving him a name was my declaration of going to war to fight for his life in any manner that I could. I would not give up on this gorgeous baby chimpanzee. He deserved the fight for life and he deserved a name.

The first thing we did after we purchased him was to take him to a vet. The vet said he would never survive because he had diarrhea and dysentery. The life prognosis for Charley was near zero.

The vet didn't even want to give Charley an IV since he felt there was no hope and it would be a waste of money. So we took this suffering chimpanzee home and we decided to treat him like a sick baby human. And with quite zero knowledge on how to take care of a baby chimp we began treating him just like a human by giving him gentle tea in a bottle and enriched liquids.

Charley wasn't making any moves. The only sign of life was a sad, empty, look in his eyes. Those eyes told us of all the misery he was feeling and went through to get there. He was sad to death. So, with every second, we were giving Charley all the liquids he could take and all the affection he was missing. For the first few days Charley spent 90% of his time in our arms.

We could tell that the only improvement was in his eyes. It was a look that kept asking for help and being thankful for all of the care he was getting. We could tell that he wanted to live. It was a human and loving look.

We got so attached to him that we were ready to do anything, anything to make him live. We prayed, we spent every night up with him, and we researched everything we could to learn how to take care of him better. After only ten days, Charley started having real food; solid food; like fruits and vegetables. After two weeks, he was able to sit up by himself.

All that time, Charley was living in our home with us. After a month, Charley was stronger; he was sitting, crawling, and playing with our kids. He began to beg for food. But, of course, he was on a diet that wasn't really pleasant to him. He became very active. He was getting his strength and health back. He became very curious. The apartment wasn't enough for Charley. There wasn't enough space for him to discover the world.

I began to take him every day to the farm. Because he wasn't fully recovered he spent most of his time in my office discovering his new surroundings but because of his young age, after half an hour or an hour of playing, Charley wanted to have a nap. He would insist on having his nap in my arms every time, which obviously wasn't very practical to me for work.

In an attempt to address this, we got him his own special little couch and we taught him to begin to use it for his naps. The couch was his place to be in the office when I had meetings. But even on the couch he would get bored or lonely. He wanted to come back to my arms so he learnt how to manipulate me. He was a very good manipulator. Anytime I asked him to go back to his couch he would start to cry and beg. This would make me look bad in front of the people I was having meetings with so I fell for it every single time. He would wind up in my arms while I held my meetings.

I never thought that one day I would get a chimpanzee or have one in my office. I never thought that one day I would have a zoo with wild animals. Each step seemed so natural and simple in its clarity. It all started with my love for animals and an idea to use animals for therapy. From there, the idea grew to create a hobby farm with the standard farm animals for the purpose of educating children. Children would come and meet the animals, they would learn about each one, learn how to take care of them, and learn about the preservation of life. It never occurred to me that one day I would be having lions, bears, panthers, or Charley to take care of.

The Journey

I didn't know that in the moment I had paid money to get Charley, I was taking the next step of an adventure that would bring me far far far away from whatever I thought my life would be. It all started in Lebanon and now I am in Canada.

The journey began when I got a collection of different kinds of chickens and birds for the purpose of therapy. I wanted to share life and the joy of innocence with the people I worked with. There was some empty land and it just made sense to build a small chicken coop.

At the same time, we were given a dog by a friend who was leaving Lebanon. Katia had always taken care of animals for her friends. They knew that we would take in their dog as they left the country.

We kept the dog at our apartment and he was a happy dog. A couple of months later, another friend brought us another dog. Now we had two dogs at the apartment. Less than two weeks later Whiskey, a kitten, joined the family.

Whiskey had some issues that were difficult to overcome. Whiskey didn't believe that heights could cause her harm so if the door to the balcony was open she would leap off. Once she broke her paw but that did not deter her from her beliefs of flight. Eventually we allowed Whiskey in and out privileges from the front door.

With a suicidal cat and a couple of dogs, the apartment began to get a little noisy. The animals were, admittedly, loud when they would play and this disturbed our neighbours. They began to complain about the noise. Since the location where I worked had plenty of space and a few animals there already I suggested to Katia that we move there. There was a small house on the property that we could take over.

Katia was not excited by the idea at all. The place was outside of town and a distance from the school where she worked. But, when we were given the third dog and the pressure from our neighbours became more serious, we had to make the decision. The children were thrilled with the idea of moving; but Katia and I, not so much. Katia would have to drive an hour to her school instead of being able to walk as she could from the apartment.

We made the move out of town and, thankfully, Katia wound up enjoying the lifestyle that being in the center of the nature offered us. The road of life is sometimes bumpy. However, the important thing is to never forget that events, crisis, and setbacks are nothing more than an opportunity. This move revealed strength and courage that we did not know resided within us. Our family bonds became so much stronger and grew from facing the challenge and overcoming it.

After awhile, I decided to start an educational farm. I always wanted to have a farm. I always wanted to live on a farm. And, as an educator, I also loved to teach and educate, so I tried to combine these two passions into one project. Living with animals and educating people on how to take care of life, all kinds of life. It made sense. We already had the birds so what could a few more barnyard animals lead to?

The farm began to grow. We had goats, sheep, cows, horses, pigeons, and our pride was our peacocks. The farm was opened for school groups to come, spend the day, and to live in the rhythm of the farm. The students would feed the animals, clean, and enjoy the farm products. Soon after the farm was open, our friends began asking us to take care of wounded animals that they found here and there.

All that started with an abandoned dog then an injured cat. We ended up having about twenty dogs on the farm, a bunch of cats, noisy parrots and, one day, a hunter brought us a grey wolf that he had shot in the leg. The wolf was so badly wounded that when we took him to the vet, the only thing that could be done to save his life was to cut off his leg, to amputate him. We wanted to save his life so we did it.

We brought him back to the farm after the operation and he wasn't able to walk. At the edge of the farm, away from all the other animals, we put him in a small cage with an open door in case he wanted to go back to the wild. We brought him food and fresh water. Two days later we were surprised to discover that another wolf had joined him, his female partner.

That day I cried. We kept the cage open after the female came, but she wouldn't leave; she wanted to stay. We decided to close the door and we built a large enclosure for the wolves. She became part of our family. She would not leave him to his fate. And this is how we ended up having a pair of grey wolves on the farm.

The way we were sheltering animals got spread out to the world; it was like a dream come true. People continuously brought hurt animals to us. One time, a hunter brought a baby fox. This fox kit was all that remained of his family. The hunter had dealt with the rest. For some reason the hunter felt something, a spark of compassion perhaps, and left the kit alive.

We took the kit in and put him in a small cage while he was recovering. The thing is, every night he was in his cage and every morning he wasn't there. Each and every single night this kit found another way to get out of his cage. We tried everything we could. We even tried using really small chicken wire but, somehow, the kit still found a way out.

He bested all of our attempts at keeping him in his cage. Nothing worked. We ended up leaving this kit to walk free and he decided to become part of our family. The moment we opened up his cage and stopped forcing him to stay, he came back by his own choice. He would ask us for food, attention, and he loved being with people. Every visitor was able to feed him and pet him.

Without meaning to and without planning it our farm became an animal shelter. Thinking back, it was normal that this would happen to us. In Lebanon there aren't laws to protect animals. We were the only place where people could go if they had any wounded animals or non-desired animals. We started having a larger variety of animals even small ones like turtles and fish. Children would even bring frogs they didn't want to our pond.

The animals began to grow more varied and exotic. One day, a family came to us and told us about a crocodile. A crocodile that they had at home in an aquarium but the crocodile was getting to big to stay in their home. They wanted us to take him. Well, of course, we said no because we had no idea on how to take care of a crocodile or where to put it. But, when we didn't agree to take it into our shelter they said something that changed our mind. They said, "Then we'll put the crocodile in the river." We realized that we couldn't allow this to happen. We reconsidered and decided to keep it. Allowing the crocodile to be released into the river would have been a double danger since he might bite someone or he may not survive.

People are often not aware of the responsibilities and commitment that they make the moment that they purchase an animal. They are unaware of the dangers that they pose for others if they mistreat their animal or decide to release the animal into the "wilderness." There is a responsibility to be a guardian for every life taken into our own lives.

From that moment we started the inside joke, "What's next? A Lion?"

 Reine

Reine was one of the first people who joined our team at the farm. She was a nurse working in the largest hospital in the emergency department. She saved so many lives but because of the bureaucracy and many issues she also lived through huge tragedies and frustrations by not being able to save so many more. She lived in greyness between her mission and the realities of the system.

We met her at the time when she was looking for answers. Looking to fully live her passion of saving lives. She was looking for a meaning. The farm was a kind of healing sanctuary for all of the despair that she was going through.

The only problem standing between Reine and her passion to what we were doing was her phobia of dogs. For whatever reason Reine was unable to approach any dog. By this time at the farm we had grown the number of adopted dogs to around a half dozen. The call of the farm was strong so even with her fear she came to help us.

Soon after Reine joined us, a family brought a cocker spaniel named Bill that they couldn't leave at home. An abandoned family dog is a dog that lives in continuous tragedy. They rarely get over it. They will mourn for their lost family and keep looking to find them. But Bill, more than any other dog I've encountered, was really devastated and sad. He stopped eating. We had to put him in a cage because from the moment the family left he showed aggressiveness towards anything that moved.

A few weeks later, we had to let Bill out of the cage because he was getting weaker and weaker from not eating well. He immediately ran towards the house and chose a corner of the living room by the fireplace as his territory. That same night, we had a late meeting with the volunteers at the house. We were very tired and one of the volunteers got excited about a subject he was discussing with Reine, and to explain his point of view he stood up in front of her.

Bill went crazy. He started growling and approached the volunteer as menacingly as he could be. We didn't understand what set Bill off. But the moment the volunteer sat down Bill went back to his corner. The meeting continued and I wanted to do some role playing. I divide everyone into two groups. I asked one of the volunteers to be a group leader and I asked Reine to be the other leader.

I asked the volunteer and Reine to stand up. I was giving them directions on where to stand and I put my hand on Reine's shoulder to guide her to exactly where I wanted her to be. Bill immediately got up and charged at us. He stood at her feet and was growling and barking at me. Of course, Reine stopped breathing. She panicked thinking Bill was attacking her.

This was when it hit us all that Bill was defending Reine. She made her way to the couch and collapsed down from fear, shaking a bit. Bill followed her and hopped up onto the couch. Bill rested his head upon Reine's lap. Reine was scared and didn't know what to do but she timidly laid her hand on Bill.

Reine, who was working to heal so many lives, was healed by a lonely and abandoned cocker spaniel. Bill became her dog. He would go home with her and would always stay by her side. Bill got a second family and confirmed for Reine that her choice to join the farm was the right one to live.

Reine was a blessing. As a nurse she was able to do injections and was able to understand the best out of all of us the directions from the vets. She had a special connection with the animals. She was amazing at creating meaningful relations with our visitors. When people came back to the facility they would ask for her. They enjoyed the way she was able to provide them with valuable information and the passion she had for the animals.

The Growth and the Animals

Junglee

Once I was sitting in my office which was near the entrance to the farm. I saw from my door a big and nice Mercedes stop in front of the office. A very well dressed lady came out of the car and walked to my office. She asked me about what we were doing and who we were. I answered and she told us, "You're the only hope left for my baby."

I wasn't aware of what she was talking about until she told me the story. She used to live in Africa and she had adopted a small baboon who had lost his mom. She brought it back with her to Lebanon. Her husband returned from Africa after a year of her living with this baboon and treating him like her baby. He told her that he wasn't willing to live with this baboon and he wouldn't come back to their house with it there.

She was in despair over the baboon. She said she was willing to do anything that we wanted if we would accept to take care of her baby. My first response was no. For two reasons, first, because I had no idea on how to take care of a monkey and second, for me, it wasn't a situation of life or death. The baboon had a home.

My daughter who was in my office with us did not agree. She was saying nothing but I could see in her look how disappointed she was in me. It was the kind of look that I wasn't able to handle. I kept talking with this lady who was trying to convince me. Finally, she said, just let me introduce my baby to you.

I said okay so she brought it from the car. The first thing this baboon did was jump on my desk, slap my face, and jump on my daughter's lap where she proceeded to hide her face from me against my daughter's chest. The lady was apologetic and explained to me that the baboon didn't like men. Her husband hadn't treated the baboon well and because of this the baboon hated men.

She explained that if we didn't take the baboon then her husband was ready to throw the baboon out. My daughter stood up with the baboon in her arms, looked at me and said, "Okay, we're keeping it. I'm going to feed it. It's my monkey."

The only thing left for me to do was to discuss with this lady all what we should know about the baboon. How to care of it, what to feed it, and all of the essentials. We adopted the baboon under the name of Junglee because, to me, the baboon had jungle manners.

This lady was an angel for us. By adopting her baby she adopted us. She was there for us so many times when we had no other avenues to go to. Unfortunately, a year later, she went back to Africa and we lost her patronage.

Aladin

At around this time I was looking for an old carriage to put at the entrance of the farm as a decorative item. On the way to Beirut with my wife we saw a man with a carriage and a horse. He had a camel as well. It seemed that he was going from the north of Lebanon to Beirut so, of course, we talked to the guy and asked if he wanted to sell the carriage.

He said he would sell it if I bought the horse as well. With the amount of money he asked for it was a good deal so I went for it. I asked him about the camel and what he was doing with it. The camel used to be in a touristic area and had grown too old. The man was bringing the camel to the city for slaughter. I felt bad for this camel who had served and brought joy to so many people. I imagined him in so many family pictures and thought it ignoble to have this kind of end to his life.

I asked him if I could buy the camel as well. The man made up his mind that I'm stupid and figured that he could get a good amount of money out of it. We fell in love with this camel and wanted to save his life. So we agreed upon the amount of money. We further agreed that he would bring all three to the farm on the next day.

Before we finished the deal, the seller said that he wanted to tell me one last thing about the camel. He told me to look over at the camel and then, without warning me, he asked the camel to kiss me. Suddenly I saw these huge lips coming at my face and it was the one of the rare moments where I got the panic of my life. I felt as if the camel was going to eat me. But he was just kissing me. This camel joined us at the farm and brought joy to many children and, probably, a few moments of panic to parents because he still likes to give kisses.

 # Tony

When Tony came and asked to work at the farm, I didn't want him. He was the kind of person who would curse between every other word he said. He was a militia guy. He had fought in the militia and lost his legs to a mine. His past was violence and war. Because of his amputation I didn't know if he would be able to work the long hours and do the heavy lifting. I was concerned for him and his constant abrasive swearing and cursing held me at bay. I said no but he came back the next day.

He told me that, "I want this. You don't understand I need this job." To put him off, I told him that I wouldn't pay him and he said he didn't care. He wanted this job. Since I really needed the help I said yes because he was persistent. I felt uncertain about the decision but said yes anyway.

Before Tony started at the farm I heard that my cousin was looking for a driver so I sent Tony to him. Tony came back to me and told me that they had offered him the job. He told me that before he would accept the other job he had a question for me. That question was, "Do you want me here?" I said well you have a great opportunity with the offer. He said he wasn't asking that. He asked me if I wanted him here.

He told me that all of his life he had been a professional soldier and this is something that he could not change. This place offered change for him. He wanted that his fight brought life rather than took it. He wanted his children to be proud of him. He wanted to be able to tell them stories that brought light to their lives and not sadness or shame. He wanted them to have a different image of him, of life, and of mankind. He was desperate to give meaning to his existence.

Of course, Tony didn't say it just like that, but that's what he was trying to say beneath all the cussing and swearing.

What changed my mind about my decision was his energy. His tenacity and his drive to live and to protect life. I realized that there was something greater than his cursing and the amputation.

I never regretted the decision of relenting and allowing Tony to open my own eyes to what people can be inside. With Tony, and because of him, we got to save so many lives on our journey. Tony ended up being one of my best zookeepers with amazing managerial skills.

Rosy the Pelican

We kept receiving calls from everywhere about small and big animals. Whenever there was a possibility to say no and we knew that the animals were safe and had other options than us we would say no. We were overwhelmed with what we already had in terms of expenses and all of the learning that we had to do just to keep up. Our only source of income was a few schools that came to visit the farm.

The few wild animals that we had, stayed out of reach and sight of the school's visits. We kept trying to put these animals back in the wild and stay with our small project of a farm and shelter.

One day, we received a call from an engineer who was building a beach resort and wanted us to come and help resolve a problem. We went to the construction site and met Rosy. Rosy was a pelican with a hint of pink in her feathers. Rosy had been living on this stretch of beach for two years since she had landed there with a wounded wing.

Her wing was broken and she was unable to fly. She had settled in and made that part of the beach her home. A fisherman there used to feed her on a regular basis. But, when they decided to build this resort the fisherman left, and Rosy became a problem. They didn't know what to do with her. The options that they thought they had was to kill and get rid of her, or for us to find her a new home. This was how we started digging out a pelican pond at the farm.

That pond that was built for Rosy became a home for swans, ducks, and other water birds came and lived there. We had seasonal visitors at the pond. Rosy seemed to attract other birds and so many water birds came through the pond.

After Rosy settled into her new pond, the joke remained, "What's next? A Lion?"

Sandy and the Mayor

We adopted another new dog at the farm. She was a husky and was sand in coloration. We decided to name her Sandy.

Sandy had bad manners. She would catch ducks from the pond and then dig a hole to bury them in alive. She was so stubborn. It was impossible to keep Sandy in an enclosure. She was capable of breaking out of any enclosure and she was so strong that she could break any chain.

The day came that I was very frustrated about not finding a solution to keep Sandy away from the ducks. It had become urgent to find Sandy a home away from the farm.

On that day when I was looking for someone to adopt Sandy we got a surprise visit from the Mayor of the village. Of course, I was there to greet him. After the introductions I asked, "To what honor do we owe your visit?"

He said, "I am here to check on Sandy and see if it bothers you to have her visiting the farm."

I was surprised by this comment but this was the mayor so I needed to be polite about Sandy. I let the mayor know that Sandy wasn't just a visitor but that this was her house. Of course, she still needed time to adapt to the farm but she would end up being good if she stopped chasing the ducks.

And with pride mixed with a bit of surprise he answered, "Who Sandy? My baby?"

I was also very surprised. It wasn't usual in Lebanon to refer to a dog as your baby. I said, "Wow! Well, Sir, I am surprised. I didn't know that Sandy was yours."

"Yes, she is mine, she is my daughter. I have another son who'd love to come here but he's a little bit young and would need an adult to visit with him."

This is when I understood that the Sandy that the mayor was talking about was not the Sandy we had adopted. To cover for my own misunderstanding, I responded with, "Oh your daughter! I'm sorry, I was confusing her with another Sandy. Your Sandy is welcome here any time and she is more than welcome to come look at the animals."

Immediately, I changed the name of our Sandy to Bella and let the entire crew know that Sandy was the name of the mayor's daughter and that it would be suicide for us to keep the husky's name Sandy. In Lebanon, it is extremely insulting to name a dog after a human. And, Mr. Mayor, if you are reading this book and you're still the mayor I hope that you can laugh about this now.

A couple of days later I found blood around Bella's mouth. I thought she had hurt herself and I cleaned up her mouth but I didn't see any cuts, scrapes, or anything. I didn't give it another thought. The next day, it was the same thing. There was blood in Bella's mouth. While doing my tour of the farm I met one of the shepherds who lived in the area and he stopped to warn me of attacks on his flock.

He told me to be sure to close the farm every evening because there was a hyena around and that it had killed two of his sheep. He said that the mayor was aware of what was happening and that a hunting party was being organized to take care of the hyena.

This is when I realized that Bella had struck again.

After this, we brought Bella to our house where she started spending the nights until we built her a very serious enclosure. She wasn't allowed to be out at night anymore.

Again, Mr. Mayor, my apologies for the trouble that Bella caused.

The Parrot

As Christmas approached I was given an early "gift" from my cousin. My cousin kept a parrot at his home but he started to get complaints from his neighbors about the noise of the bird He brought it to the farm and asked me to keep it for awhile so that his neighbors would calm down and stop telling him to get rid of it. My cousin assured me that the parrot would be quiet and that, unfortunately, the parrot couldn't speak.

Because the parrot was used to live in a house we found him a nice place in our living room. The day after we took the parrot in I was up early in the morning and making my coffee. I heard someone say, "Good morning." I looked around me but saw no one. I opened the front door to check to see if someone had come to visit but, again, there was no one there. I finished making my coffee and went to work.

The next morning it was the same thing. I heard the same, "Good morning." I searched around to see if there was anyone there but, again, found no one. When it is early in the morning and it is still dark outside there are lots of ideas in your mind about what is going on. I couldn't figure out what was going on. Maybe someone was playing a trick on me?

I went back from the kitchen to the living room feeling a bit angry. I shouted, "GOOD MORNING!" And from the corner where the parrot was the answer came, "Good morning." I was surprised because my cousin had told me that the only sound the parrot would make was a loud squawking and that the parrot couldn't say a word.

I began every day at 5 AM when my alarm would go off. The only day that my alarm wouldn't go off at 5 AM was Sunday. Sunday was my rest day. The Sunday after the parrot joined us, right on time at 5 AM, I was awakened by the sound of my alarm clock. I tried everything to shut off my clock! I hit snooze, I pressed the buttons, I hit it, I unplugged it, I tried everything but the alarm kept going. As I became more awake I realized that the sound wasn't coming from the alarm clock so I followed the sound.

There, in his corner, was the parrot happily making the alarm sound. When he saw me, he said, "Good morning!" followed by the sound of the alarm. He was happy but I wasn't. I knew that I had one week to find a solution if I wanted to be able to sleep in the next Sunday.

My wife had gotten up as well from the alarm and followed me. She turned to me and said that the house was no longer a place for animals. I agreed with her and we moved the parrot to the farm.

 Python

Every year at this time, around Christmas, we would build a huge nativity scene in our living room. We went all out. We used wood, burlap, and hay. It would take about a week to build.

This year was no different. We had built the scene in our living room but, this year, things would work out differently. A couple of days before Christmas a family came to the farm. They had with them a three meter (almost ten feet) long python. They hoped that we could keep the snake at the farm since they were leaving the country the next day and they couldn't find anyone who would keep the snake.

Pythons are cold blooded creatures and need a warm environment to stay. Since it was near Christmas and the temperature outside was cold there weren't a lot of options on where to have the python stay. We had no place at the farm that would be able to house the python properly. Plus, I had a fear of snakes, the full blown phobia known as Ophidiophobia.

And yet, with all of these reasons not to take the python I couldn't say no knowing that if I didn't they would just throw the snake anywhere and leave it. They had no other solution, they were leaving, and the python wouldn't be able to survive outdoors in the winter. I said that we would take it.

They had the python in a bag so we transferred it from the bag into a large bucket. We used a piece of wood to cover the top and on top of the cover we put a brick so the snake couldn't get out. We put the bucket in the living room at the opposite side of the nativity scene.

The next morning, when I woke up at 5 AM, I walked immediately to check on the snake. The first thing I saw was that the cover was shifted by about two to three inches. I approached the bucket cautiously to check on the python through the opening. I couldn't see anything. I moved the cover further and, to my surprise and horror, the bucket was empty. The python was free in my house.

The first thing I did was run to the rooms of the children to check on them. The first door to their hallway was open. I felt my heart beating against my chest and pounding. I was panicking. The second door to the hallway where their rooms were was closed. Plus, each of their doors were closed. I checked on the kids and I realized that I had opened the doors to get there so, of course, the python wasn't there. I went back downstairs and carefully closed all the doors behind me.

I decided to make my coffee and to wait for the staff members to arrive. When they arrived we all began the search. The first place that came to my mind where the python could be was behind the nativity scene. After checking under the furniture we began removing the scene that took us about a week to build. No python was there.

To me, this was the only place where it was possible for the python to be. We continued the search and looked everywhere even beneath the fridges and all the appliances. It was about four in the afternoon when we took a break from the searching. We had looked in impossible places and we were sure that the python was still in the house but where?

My wife told me that we were not sleeping in the house as long as the python was in the house. What scared me the most was that the python was large enough to strangle one of the kids.

We took up the search again and, at around seven in the evening, we decided to have another break for some coffee and a bit to eat. We tried to figure out if there was any corner of the house that we hadn't looked at. We thought about a small space above the bathroom where the hot water tank was but discounted it because there wasn't any way up. That is, until I went to the bathroom, and saw that there was a small gap above the toilet. Seeing that hole, I knew that that was where the python had gone.

We got a ladder and put it against the wall to check the water tank. This is where I found the python. She had followed the heat and was curled up beneath the hot water tank. We debated on how to bring the python and down everybody backed up. Nobody wanted to touch the python. There was no way around it, I had to do it.

I put on an oven mitt and I went up the ladder. I tried to reach the snake. The moment that my hand approached she hissed and she attacked. I fell off the ladder from fear and shock. I sat down on the ground and we debated what the best thing to do was. I tried to climb up again but the moment I reached up with my hand she tried to strike again but couldn't reach. I waved my hand a couple of times in front of the opening and she lunged each time without reaching.

That gave me an idea. I would wave my oven mitt protected hand in front of the opening and grab the python with my other hand as she lunged for the mitt. It worked. We had a bag ready and I stuffed the python in the bag. She struggled ferociously but I wouldn't let go. I had my fear in my hand and I wasn't going to let her go until she was safely in the bag. We got her into the bag after a long struggle. The next day, we had a builder come and he built her a large terrarium. I don't need to tell you what my wife thought about this.

Chris and Jenny

Because we lived at the farm it was inevitable that my children, Chris and Jenny, would become involved with what was going on. After all, there were cute animals and lots of things to do. This was a life of adventure where their backyard was a farm. Almost every day we welcomed a new furry resident.

They were the most excited about everything happening in the farm. At a young age they learned to celebrate life and how to face the tragedy of death. Chris and Jenny brought valuable insights to the whole project.

So many times we had to face decisions where we were obliged to make a practical decision. Sometimes we had to say no to a new animal because we didn't have the money or enough knowledge to take care of it. But our thoughts would go immediately to how Chris and Jenny would react when they found out that we refused to welcome an animal in need. Every time this thought pushed us to make impractical decisions but, at the same time, these were the right decisions to make.

Chris and Jenny were incredible with the animals. Many animals that came to the farm with an aggressive attitude connected with Chris and Jenny. This gave those animals a sense of safety and security, which allowed them to drop their guard and settle in. Chris and Jenny had no fears or reservations when approaching an animal and, surprisingly, the animals would respond in the same way.

The most valuable thing that my children brought to the farm and then the zoo was the connection that other children could make through them. The visiting children were able to identify with Chris and Jenny. They were the best ambassadors to their peers. They made the animals and life real to the other children. They were the youngest zookeepers in the world.

Micho

The joke of a lion at the farm remained until the day that the local police called us. A western European zoo that was visiting the city went bankrupt and left the country, leaving behind them some animals. The police urged us to come because a few accidents had happened with the animals and now the animals were left unattended.

We went there and discovered some dogs, a pony, and an old but magnificent lion. That lion was kept in a box container with the front of the container being bars. There were a lot of people around the container throwing stones at the lion so he was extremely agitated and aggressive. We knew from the police that there had been at least two accidents with the lion. The lion had bitten a leg of one person and the hand of another.

We asked the police to clear the area. We moved the small animals to a truck and back to the farm. To move the lion, I decided that we would use a crane to lift the cage onto a truck . . . I asked the police to be left alone with the lion because I wanted to find a way to calm him down and to feed him before we did the transfer. I wanted to make the moving the least bit stressful as possible.

At this moment the lion was so agitated. He was roaring and pacing and really upset. I was left alone with the lion in front of the cage. I knew the lion's name from the sign on his cage, it said Micho. I crouched down before the cage and started to say his name quietly. I didn't know what else to say or what to do. It wasn't real for me since this was the first time I had ever seen a lion. I knew that we were the only solution for that lion but I didn't know how to make it happen. This was the joke becoming reality.

All I did was repeat his name softly while waiting for the crane. After a little while, I started talking to Micho promising to take care of him but also sharing with him my worries about not knowing what to do next. Micho suddenly calmed down and began to stare at me as if he were listening. I told him that I wanted him to be calm and to give me a chance to take care of him promising him that I was going to provide him with a decent life. Micho watched me with his huge eyes and then he lay on his back and gave me his throat just like a small cat asking me to pet him.

It was magic. I slowly put my hand through the bars towards him. As I did, I wondered if I was going to reach him or if I was going to lose my hand just like the guy the police had told me about. But, I think that at that moment, a special kind of bond was born between me at this amazing creature.

In silence and in a moment of dreamlike quality my hand reached him. It was like my hand was detached from my body. I wasn't conscious of what I was doing. There was a primal attraction that wrapped us in the moment. It was just the right thing to do. The moment my hand touched his chin he closed his eyes. I pet him for maybe five minutes and then everyone else arrived.

We were able to move Micho without incident. At the farm, Micho lived for about two weeks in his small cage while we built a much larger enclosure off of the back of his container. During this time we did as much research as we possibly could to learn everything about lions. Micho settled in quietly and was kept out of sight of our visitors.

After Micho's arrival everyone knew when I was coming onto the grounds because Micho would roar the moment he felt my approach. I used to travel often, for instance to France, to learn about wild animals, and even when I was gone for a week on the day that I was back everyone knew I was coming because Micho felt my presence. "Felt my presence" is an understatement, the moment I came within a kilometer of the facility he would stand up at his cage, his paws on the bars, and begin to roar. I would still be in my car and couldn't see the entrance but, somehow, Micho knew I was coming.

Every morning I had a routine: when I was done with my inspections I would go to Micho and brush him and pet him for about ten minutes. It's amazing how this all turned out. When we were contacted about Micho they qualified him as a ferocious man-killer. If we hadn't taken him they were going to put him down. He turned out to be a loving creature.

We also had rabbits. One day these rabbits found a way to escape from their enclosure. We rounded them up and recaptured them but we were still missing a white rabbit. When the team was feeding the animals in the afternoon they called me panicking. They found the white rabbit in Micho's enclosure. I went to the cage to try and find a way to get the rabbit out from the cage.

It was amazing. The lion was sitting as he normally did and the rabbit was sitting between his paws. They were relaxing together. We couldn't do anything and we thought this would be the end of the little creature's life. We guessed that the rabbit was so scared that he couldn't move and Micho was going to eat him. The next day in the morning during my usual routine I checked Micho's cage and saw the lion but not the rabbit.

However, in the afternoon, the rabbit was back in the same position between Micho's paws. We brought some carrots for the rabbit to try and get him to approach the fence so we could pull him out. He grabbed the carrots but immediately hopped back to Micho where he ate his carrots. This situation became a ritual that was filmed on the national TV and shown on prime time news.

People used to come and see this lion and rabbit living together.

Micho's enclosure had a double fence. An inner fence and an outer fence. I would walk between the two fences and talk about him to the visitors. During the presentation I would walk close to Micho's cage and he would rub against the bars so I could pet him. Once during my presentation, my daughter who was watching my guided tour, screamed. I turned around quickly, alarmed to see what was wrong. Jenny called out that I had to be careful because there was a bee near me and it may sting me.

Micho stayed with us for six years. On the sixth year, I will never forget his last day. Every night when I did my night inspection to make sure all the animals were taken care of properly before I left. I always finished my round at Micho's cage. We used to have this small game where I would "ignore" him and pass his cage. He would stand up on his hind feet and roar at me to call me over. I would go back, pet him for a few moments under his chin, and then I would leave.

That night I did the same thing that I always did. I finished my inspection and Micho roared. But this time he didn't stand. When I went back to his cage he was laying on the floor, giving me his throat, like the first day I met him. I pet his chin and called him a lazy old lion then stood up to leave. Once I was beyond his sight he roared again. This was the first time that he did it twice. I went back, pet him again, and told him I had to go home.

He did it a third time. That time I told him to stop it because he's getting spoiled and even if he called me again I wouldn't come back since I had to go home. So I left Micho roaring and calling for me. I ignored it as I said I would but I could still hear him by the time I got to my car.

The next morning, on my way in I received a phone call from one of the keepers telling me that they found Micho dead in his cage. This is when I understood that Micho was saying goodbye and, maybe, thank you. I felt as if I had just lost a dear friend. I will always remember Micho and what joy he brought to our lives.

The Transformation from Farm to Zoo

With the arrival of all these animals our expenses were getting to be very large. The cost of the food alone for all of our animals was significant. We needed a way to get our name out there since we needed more resources.

Our original idea and what we worked for had been the establishment of an educational farm. A place where people with disabilities could find therapeutic activities, and also for the public, an educational environment where they could learn about the richness of animal life and conservation. With all the wounded animals that we started welcoming, a big part of the farm became a shelter where visitors were not allowed. This way we could protect the animals and people.

Somehow we were sure that these animals were there only temporarily. They were waiting to be set free when they were ready. It was a completely new world for us that we were not prepared to handle. With time we accepted the sad reality that some of these animals would not be able to live by themselves in the wild anymore.

With the number of animals growing we started to become affected by the cruelty that these animals suffered before coming to us. We decided to adopt this cause and to defend it. A new journey began for us. We ended up opening the shelter to visitors for two main reasons and both reasons were vital to us.

The first was to generate enough money that we urgently needed to keep going to be able to offer the care that the growing number of animals needed. We needed the money to support what the shelter had become. We were broke. We had no money to feed the animals. The members of the crew were managing by getting the minimum for the animals. Our people weren't being paid so they started to leave.

The second one was to create a hands-on awareness campaign. The word shelter was not a commonly used word back then. We advertised the project as a zoo to attract the largest number of people.

Once they arrived the first thing that they would see was a welcoming sign reading, "This is a shelter not a zoo." The sign went on to explain our vision and our mission.

We didn't want an entrance fee, we wanted to make it about awareness. We tried, for a brief time, to allow people to visit our animal shelter for free and let people donate. But, unfortunately, most people came, watched, and left. Once we realized that we couldn't support ourselves in this manner we were forced to add in an entrance fee. We wanted to be affordable for everyone so we set the fee to be $2 per person. We still accepted donations.

Why $2? We didn't want to become a commercial activity and only focus on profit. We wanted people to understand that we opened our zoo to support the animals. We decided on the entrance fee based on what was fair and honest concerning the work we did and what our mission was. For $2 we weren't going to make a profit but we would be able to cover the basic needs of the animals.

The most cost effective way for us to start getting people to come and to pay was to create brochures. We didn't have enough money to pay for distribution from a professional company. Instead, my son used to walk by foot to place brochures in any store nearby that would accept them and our other team members would drive out to further neighborhoods to advertise.

We still barely had enough to feed the animals. With animals there are always problems, there is always a need for vets, vitamins, and food. Once we had a reliable source of money we were able to pay more attention to the residents of the farm and provide the service that they needed to have. We sought out specialist vets, bought healthier food, got more vitamins, and improved the enclosures.

I started to travel more and more to find out as much as I could about the animals, how to house them, and where to keep them. I traveled to France, Germany, Belgium, Greece, Cyprus, and several other countries to generate new connections and expand my knowledge.

At the same time, people were getting to know us better by visiting us and through our advertising. The word about our shelter was out, and people brought us even more animals. This meant more and more expenses and we wanted to treat every animal properly. Because we had some resources behind us it was harder for us to say no. The expectation was greater now. People expected us to help the animals since we had become the professionals.

We started an adoption program for abandoned pets. Instead of buying a dog people could come and adopt a dog from the zoo. They would go through a background check and screening before we

Joseph M. Daccache

made them sign papers. After the process they could take the dog home. This program was very successful so we began a sponsorship program where people could sponsor an animal at the zoo.

For this program, the people who sponsored animals received advantages such as when there was a new birth we would invite them to get the first look. We had a monthly newsletter to keep all of our sponsors informed as to what was going on at the zoo. We explored every option that we could think of to bring money to the zoo to cover its growing needs without changing our focus away from the animals. We wanted the best for our animals.

Introduction to the Zoo

The zoo wasn't really a zoo. It was conceived to be a temporary habitat for abandoned animals so they could have a shelter until they got stronger and could find a permanent resident. For those animals that were wounded, it was a place to receive the necessary care to be able to heal and head out once more.

We discovered that opening to the public with an entrance fee not only generated income would give us the opportunity to meet with a bigger number of people so we could educate and create awareness regarding the protection of animals and the importance of these creatures in the balance of our planet.

Amongst our visitors we had some directors of media, like TV, radio, and newspaper and they gave us the opportunity to use their mediums so we could bring the spotlight onto the problems of animal abuse. We even had a weekly radio show where we discussed different subjects. In a country where the human life was violated, where people were missing basic things like security, talking about animal protection might seem ridiculous. But, despite this situation, surprising as it was people showed compassion and were understanding.

Their excitement went beyond our expectation. We began to receive calls and offers for help. Through this, we noticed something very important about people; the ones who gave the most were often the ones who had the least. The more people contemplated death the more they wanted to protect life especially the weakest forms of life. War can take everything away from you, your life and the lives of your loved ones, nevertheless, it cannot take the humanity out of the people.

 # Animal Stories at the Zoo

Leopards

With our opening as a zoo more people became aware of us. Because of this we received a phone call from the airport customs. They had impounded two strange kinds of cats at the airport when they had arrested a smuggler from Tanzania. They wanted me to check it out and see what these two cats were.

Once I arrived, they opened up the cages and showed me the felines; I was surprised to see two beautiful leopards. I told them what they were and they asked me how to care for them. We gave them some water, I brought them some meat, and we left.

Two days later, we received another phone call from customs, informing us that they were unable to send the leopards back to their country of origin and that we had to find a home for them. For us, it was a big problem we had never had such wild cats before. Micho had grown up in captivity. These two cats were straight from the wild.

We quickly built a "temporary" home for these two leopards. Since the two leopards were a male and a female and had arrived together we put the two of them in the same enclosure. We kept the leopards under observation.

We noticed that the female was getting bigger and the male seemed weak. We figured that he wasn't getting any of the food and she was taking it all. We weren't sure because, at that time, they weren't used to people and they never ate in front of us. Instead, they would wait until no one was around.

To solve the problem, we called the welder to build another cage and we separated the cats at night. During the day they were together and at night they would have separate homes. This way we knew that both cats were getting enough food. A couple of days later during my regular early morning inspection round I was surprised to see another leopard in with the female. Sweety was born.

Unfortunately, we believe that since the birth took place in captivity, the mom wasn't feeding her. We spent the whole night watching her and she wasn't approaching her baby. We thought we were going to lose the newborn. We pulled Sweety out and we started to hand feed her using a bottle. And, of course, I had to take her home with me so we could feed her every few hours.

Sweety lived at home for about seven months and used to join us for all our family trips since we couldn't leave her unattended. She was very sweet and very playful. But Sweety had a disease. A problem where her back legs didn't function properly. There were times when she could not use her hind quarters at all.

We started bringing her to our local vet to see if he could figure it out. Our vet was a farm animal vet but he contacted other vets at other zoos to see what could be done. He ran a lot of tests and worked really hard at finding a solution. He found a medication that might work for her condition and we gave her the pills with every meal.

At this time, my daughter was in charge of Sweety's bathing. Jenny was eight and during one of the panther's weekly baths she "accidentally," as she tells me now, used black dye instead of shampoo. This dye turned Sweety's fur all black. It was a kind of henna dye and harmless. We laughed about it and didn't give it much thought because we knew that it would fade in a couple of weeks.

We sent Sweety for her regular check-up to the vet with the farm manager. The vet called me to let me know that he wanted to keep Sweety for a few days to observe her. I called him two days later to see if we could get her back but he told me that he still needed more time. He sounded worried.

When he had found out about the treatment he was told that this kind of disease could kill Sweety which was why we didn't question his keeping Sweety. We were afraid that the treatment wasn't working and that the vet was keeping her to do what he could.

Two or three days later he called me and by his voice I could tell that he had good news. He sounded relieved. He told me that he had one good one bad news. The good news was that the treatment was working very well and there were no lives threatening reactions.

But, the bad news was that there was a side effect that he had been trying to figure out all week long. He had conferred with his colleague in France and still had no answer on why the treatment was affecting the pigmentation of her fur. The treatment was causing her fur to turn black.

I laughed so hard that it took me a few minutes to form a sentence. I got about twenty "Why are you laughing?" questions from the vet and, finally, once I could speak again I told him the real reason why Sweety's fur was black. How a child's mischief made so many doctors wonder about a revolutionary medication they had such high hopes for.

When Sweety reached seven months in age she got so active that we put her in her own enclosure where she settled in nicely without problems.

Donations and Sponsors

The animal shelter was a place of daily miracles. We never had abundance and rarely did we have in advance what we would need. But, somehow we always received the resources that we needed just in time. This would not have been possible without the presence and the help of a lot of people.

Whenever you decide to fulfil a dream the whole universe comes together to help you. When we needed help the world delivered it to us miraculously at the right moment. Whatever it was that we needed, a helping hand, a thousand dollars, tens of thousands, it arrived when it was needed. Of course, we had to put in all the hard work and live through the challenges to go over so many obstacles but this is what got people to believe in us. Our dedication and devotion made them willing to help us with their time, expertise, and money.

Everyone had their own reason and motivation to help but what was common to everyone was their love of life and willingness to be a part of this journey to protect and promote the culture of life. In the darkest of moments they brought light and hope. Because of this sacred commitment that we had I am still fighting to keep going and continue the battle.

One example stands out to me. We saw that Micho's urine was pink so we immediately brought in a vet. We discovered that Micho needed surgery because the vet thought it may be testicular cancer. For that we needed $12,000 USD. We did not have that kind of money sitting in any type of reserve. This stressful situation made us really sad. It was a disaster knowing that Micho was going to die because we didn't have money.

That evening we had a birthday party at the zoo. At the end of the birthday the father came to thank me for the amazing time that they had. He offered his help if we needed anything for the zoo. I grabbed the opportunity and I told him about Micho's health issues. He showed a lot of compassion and left.

The next day, I was in a meeting with the whole staff trying to brainstorm on how to find a way to raise money to save Micho. $12,000 USD was a huge fortune for us. I was told that someone was on the phone for me. It was the birthday guy. It turned out that he worked for the company Nestle. He had spoken to his marketing manager and they were willing to offer us the $12,000 for Micho's operation. We asked them what they wanted in return and they said nothing! We offered to put on Micho's enclosure a plaque with a small story about how Nestle saved Micho's life. They accepted only because we insisted. For us, it was important to let people know for educational awareness and for encouragement that anyone can make a difference.

We wanted this project to be one where we celebrate life. We wanted people to see how they, too, could help to protect and promote life. This is why an event like this was so important to talk about. People never seemed to miss a chance to tell stories about how people harm one another or harm animals. We wanted to take this opportunity to show them how one company reached out and offered to save the life of an animal for nothing in return. This is the story we wanted to tell and it was important for us to do so.

Dingo Sponsor

We used to have neighbours and these neighbours kept complaining about having the zoo next door and in their area. They would complain to the health authorities and send them after us. We never had a problem with the health authorities but they kept sending them. We got to know the people at the department of health very well and liked them a lot.

One summer day, our neighbour's threw a huge wedding party and something much unexpected happened. The neighbour's sister happened to be not only the bride but also an animal activist. During the celebration she heard about the problems her family was having with the neighbouring zoo. She was so excited to come and visit that she decided to bring the entire bridal party over that day.

After a tour at the zoo, she fell in love with what we were doing. She decided to help us with whatever we needed. At that time, we were preparing ourselves to receive Dingo, a bear. The only thing that was holding us back from being able to bring Dingo in was the lack of funding to build an enclosure for such a big animal. She offered the money to build the enclosure of around five thousand dollars.

What did we need the five thousand for? We needed to build an enclosure strong and big enough for the big bear to be safe and to keep everybody else safe.

A week before this bridal event happened we had received a call from the local police telling us that a worker came to them with a complaint against his employer. He worked at an orange orchard and the owner kept a small cage with a big bear in it near the back of his farm and the owner had stopped taking care of the bear and had asked the worker to find a way to feed it without buying him any food and provided no money to purchase any anyway.

The only way the worker could feed the bear was to give him the left over oranges from the trees. It had been three days since he had run out of oranges. He had no money, no oranges, and no food. The bear was starving and was beginning to break out of his small cage. The police requested that we go and see Dingo.

What we found and saw was horrible. Dingo was a grizzly bear living in a two square meter cage. No shed, no privacy, no shelter, and living in his own mess because no one would clean the cage. All day, every day, in the sun or in the rain with no shelter. Dingo was throwing himself against the cage walls trying to break out.

After trying to escape, many times he would roll on the floor with screams of anguish and agony. It wasn't hope, it was pure despair. When we took a closer look we saw that he was suffering from a skin disease. He was losing his fur and his skin. This environment was revolting. At the same time we didn't know what we could do. He was a big animal. We would need a huge cage, a strong cage, and lots of food. The only thing we were able to do on the spot was to collect money from each other and buy him some food.

We got him apples, fish, and lots of honey. We helped the workers to clean the floor and Dingo by using a hose. It wasn't ideal but it was the only thing that we were able to do at that time. We had to throw the food into the cage because there was no other way to get it to him. After we fed him, Dingo sounded calmer and more peaceful; he lay down and collapsed from exhaustion with his back towards us. We promised him that his life would get better and his environment healthier.

On our way back to the zoo we discussed the situation. We knew how clueless we were and how we couldn't afford to offer anything to save Dingo's life. We began to call the people we knew to raise some money. The only money we were able to get was barely enough to buy Dingo his daily diet. We would bring it to him every day in his miserable cage. To try and improve the cage's liveability and ambiance we put up some shade and we paid the worker to clean it on a daily basis.

When the bride offered us money she was also offering a new life for Dingo. Without losing a second we hired four teams of builders to work twenty-four hours non-stop to build Dingo a new home at the zoo.

About ten days from the day that we first met Dingo we were able to bring him to the zoo to begin a new life. We knew close to nothing about his past history. But we were in charge of offering him a better future. Because of Dingo we had another reason to honor life.

What we used to do on these occasions was to invite all of the sponsors and tell the story. We'd have a meal together or a drink together and we would celebrate the joy of life while wondering what would come next.

Hunters

From the commencement of this adventure, we had hunters visiting us and bringing wounded animals. But, as we grew some of them began asking for money. At first, we used to give them a part of what they asked because we were naive and wanted to save the animals then we figured out that we were encouraging these people to purposefully go out and hunt and then bring the animals in for money. So, we began to say no and we were rude to them. We would throw them out of the office. But, I figured out that this was not the solution. This wasn't about me and it wasn't about them. This was all in the way that they perceived the animals and what they were doing.

From their perspective, they weren't doing anything wrong. Throwing them out or refusing them wasn't changing anything. So I decided to try a different approach. I would try to engage the hunters the same way that we did at school with children.

We had observed that every time a school came to our zoo for the first time most children would do the same thing when we introduced the first animal. They put their arms up like they had a gun and would pretend to shoot the animal. Then, by the end of the tour, after introducing each and every animal by their name and telling their story the children would leave talking about the animals by their names. They would promise to come back with food the next time.

In the span of an hour the attitude of the children had shifted from that of a hunter to one of a protector.

This is what I began to do with the hunters that came to my office and tried to sell me animals that they hunted. I would offer them coffee and then give them a personal tour of the zoo. On the tour I would introduce each animal by their name and tell their story. As we went through the tour a shift would come upon the hunters. The moment of change, that moment of clarity when I saw the attitude shift visibly, was when I showed the living energy that resides in every living creature. What you only see when you look into the eyes of a living animal.

I used to ask them to compare this vibrant living energy with the dullness in the eyes of an animal that they just shot. By the end of the tour, the hunters, all of them, had shifted their attitude from trying to sell me to "Oh my God, I had no idea I was causing so much harm." Most of the hunters would return to the zoo regularly but not as hunters trying to sell me one of their animals anymore but as volunteers and friends of the zoo. All of them offered us donations to keep us going in our mission of offering life to animals. They were our best ambassadors next to the children.

Family Life at the Zoo

Life at the zoo was always an adventure and a story. Living on the premises meant that the stories of the animals were really our stories and our life.

My wife was a teacher, so every morning she would go with the children to school. Our children went to the same school where my wife taught. Once they were back from school everyone would put on their zoo clothing and do their daily assignments. We couldn't afford a lot of workers so we all shared in the work.

After dinner we had our family time followed by evenings spent with the members of the team and with the zoo. We formed one large family. We shared the meals, the work, and the worries. The most important thing that we shared was the dream and vision.

Joseph M. Daccache

The dream of creating a sanctuary for the unwanted and wounded animals.

We were always short on money at the zoo. So many times my wife's salary was used to help us out at the zoo. All of her bonuses and every bit of extra went into the zoo. For my children it was a dream life that they were living.

Prince

One day, one of my son's new teachers approached my wife and asked to have a private conversation regarding my son. The teacher began to tell my wife about my son's fertile imagination. She was beginning to worry about how my son was starting to confuse his imagination as reality. My wife inquired why she was saying this and the teacher told her that my son kept telling her that he lived at home with a lion.

The only thing my wife was able to do was laugh and tell the teacher that it wasn't imagination but it was, in fact, our reality. We had a baby lion at home. The teacher shook her head in disbelief and left thinking that the whole family needed to seek help. I know this because the teacher shared her thoughts with us years later.

My daughter never had that problem with her teachers because by that time everyone knew about the zoo. But, as we all know, children can be mean and jealous. Later on, my daughter let us know that some of the children told her that she smelled like animals. But both of my children were so in love with the zoo that it didn't affect any of their commitment or self-esteem.

What about the baby lion who lived with us? It was one of the saddest ways we ever met an animal that needed our help. His name was Prince.

Prince came to us through a smuggler. He had a wooden box that was fairly small and he wanted to sell us a baby lion. I was curious to see what he really had in the box. I looked into the air holes and the only thing that I could see was red. There a small form that was covered in blood. I was full of rage. This guy told me that he stole this animal from his mom, from a zoo and brought it to us. The only thing I wanted to do at the time was to call the authorities.

I asked the guy to wait because I had to confer with my team members. I went to call the police. When I came back to my office the guy was gone and there was only the box on the floor. I believe that the smuggler figured out what was going on and ran away before he could get in any trouble with the law.

We took the box and opened it slowly. There was a tiny lion cub inside. The cub was covered with blood from trying to escape the box. He had no fur on his face or on his paws. From the look of him he had some kind of skin disease as well.

We opened the box and put the opened box in an empty room. We put some food and water near the box then closed the door to the room and watched from outside. After a few hours he struggled to crawl out of the box to reach the water. He took some water and stopped moving. We were wondering what to do so we called the vet.

The vet came and shot the cub with a tranquilizer dart so he could do a full inspection. After doing the check-up, the vet told us that Prince was extremely weak and had very little chance at life. If we wanted to try to keep Prince alive we would have to use a medicated cream on his skin using a special brush twice a day. We would also have to give him pills in his food every day. The vet had stitched up Prince's paws and we needed to apply an antibiotic cream on the stitches as well.

And still, with all of the treatments, the vet didn't think that Prince would survive. The last thing he told us before leaving was that it wouldn't be worth the stress, exhaustion, and emotional burden to try. But, to us, not trying wasn't an option. If there is life there is hope. We were willing to do anything so long as there was the smallest flicker of success to keep this lion cub alive.

The next day, Prince was awake but unable to move. We had set the food plate just in front of his paws and Prince had his head between his paws. But Prince wasn't even able to move his head that small distance. I decided to intervene and assist Prince with getting his food. The moment that I opened the door and entered the room Prince began to hiss at me.

Immediately, I crouched down and stayed in place. I didn't move so Prince could get used to my presence in the room. After a long while of remaining still, I began to move slowly towards Prince. There was about three meters (twelve feet) between the door and Prince and it took about an hour to get to him. When I came within arm's length I reached out with the soft brush and touched Prince very gently while I was speaking quietly to him.

When I touched Prince with the brush, he panicked and began to hiss. I pulled the brush away for a few moments and then touched him again. I did it over and over very softly until he got used to the motion and calmed down. I brushed him for a few seconds and then I crawled back.

I repeated this same routine every hour and every time I would brush him for a longer time. The third time I did it I put some of his medical cream on the brush. Every time he would repeat his hissing and then allow me to do it. By the end of the day, I was able to go from my corner to his corner in a few seconds and brush him for about ten minutes without hissing. He would just turn his head and allow me to brush his entire body. But, he still would not eat.

The next day, I decided to touch Prince with my hand instead of the brush to try and create a bond. The first couple of times I approached I used the brush and then touched him for one second with my hand just to get him used to my touch. Every time that I did it he would flinch. I withdrew when he flinched. Each time I went to touch I would sing the same song.

The third time, as I began to sing, I waited longer before petting him. He seemed to be waiting for the touch and when I touched him he didn't flinch. I pet his back for about a minute. This happened in the middle of the day.

We needed to feed him since he hadn't eaten at all. He was getting weaker and weaker. We tried different meats, milk, everything we could think of. We had the food plate as close to him as possible without putting it inside of him but he refused to eat. We were at a loss on what we could do.

This is when it occurred to me that maybe what works with children would work with Prince. What we would do with children who refused to eat was to make a game out of it. So I went into his room and with my hand I played with a piece of meat in front of his nose. After awhile, he began to get angry and attacked the piece of meat. He ate.

I pushed the plate with meat on it because he got the taste but he still refused to eat from it. So, again, I used my hand and played with the meat in front of him. It worked again. He took the meat. This is how I had to feed Prince for about a week. Every day, four times a day, I would brush him and feed him.

Meanwhile, Prince still wasn't moving. He remained weak and unable to move. After a week, I figured out that I had to stop feeding him with my hand and had to get him to start moving. I put the food on a stick and every time he tried to bite it I moved it farther away so he had to reach. This is how he began to start crawling towards the food. Then, instead of taking it away, I began to lift it higher into the air. This forced him to stand on his feet to take the food. With the medication and with this trick he got healthier and stronger.

10 days later, the vet came back for a visit. He couldn't believe what he saw. Prince was able to walk around the room, he had a good appetite, and was playful. It was a miraculous phenomenon. A recovery the doctor had never seen before. However, Prince still needed a lot of attention and medication. I didn't mention it previously, but the room we kept him in was at our house. That's where my kids got their story from. We had a lion cub living with us at home.

Prince lived with us for about two months. When he got strong enough we moved him to his new home at the zoo. Even when he got healthier and didn't need it anymore he kept asking for his daily brushing routine.

The Rhythm at the Zoo

To me, nothing is more beautiful than living in the rhythm of nature. It is living day by day, living in the moment, and living fully with the difficulties and joys that come with life. Welcoming the start of every day with an excitement and anticipation of the unknown and the challenges that come with it. Saying that we lived a dream life and we saw the realization of it every day is not exaggeration.

I can say that every moment exceeded our every expectation. Working at the zoo wasn't a job it was a lifestyle. We never got tired or ever had enough of what we were doing. Being bored was never an issue. Sometimes we were exhausted but we still wanted to do more.

Every arrival of a new animal, always motivated the crew. A new birth brought exaltation. Everything was a reason for us to get together and to celebrate. It was a place of continual celebration of joy and life.

What gave us the greatest sense of accomplishment and joy was to bring an animal back to the wild. None of us started as experts in animal care. None of us had experience working with animals in this way. But, every one of us had a burning desire to learn and we took joy in returning animals to their natural habitat.

For the problems we could not solve, we always consulted with an expert. With every new animal we welcomed, we researched everything there was to know about our new addition, so we could learn to take care it the proper way. Calling a vet could never provide us with all that we needed to know. In Lebanon, we didn't have zoos or animal shelters so our vet was mainly specialized in farm animals. Exotic animals were a relative unknown.

Taking care of an animal was not just about giving it medication; it was about knowing their mode of life.

It's true that a cage is not the ideal place for an animal. No living creature is supposed to live in one permanently. But, when a cage is a necessary evil, there are a minimum set of qualifications needed for the comfort and well-being of its occupant. These depend on the animal's behavior, conduct, and habits. Space, exposure to sun, shelter, and some toys, were some of the criteria one had to take into account when building an enclosure. All of this is done to try and make the cage as livable as possible and not for it to become a prison.

Most of our animals came to us in emergencies. We had little time to prepare in advance and a few seconds to make the decision to keep them or not. After that, we often had mere hours to create their new habitat. With every new arrival, followed many sleepless nights.

Resources were not taken into consideration when welcoming in a new animal. It was their need for us. We would answer the call of help and then we would try to find the means to cover the costs. This was not always the best managerial attitude or behaviour but we were not business people. We were trying to save lives and diminish suffering.

We were disarmed when we faced the silent pain and misery of a living creature. There could be no alternative than to take the animal in and do what we could to improve the remainder of its life. The silent suffering was a piercing cry for help that shattered any resolve of indifference. It was a call where no excuse could stand.

Even if we had no material stored up, we managed to live day by day based on the unfailing generosity of the people around us. With time, we learned to never be afraid of not having the means available at the moment. With the rising of the sun each day we would meet new friends and gain new resources. The resources were scant at times but we never felt their lack because the dream was so fulfilling. We were crazy but we were also happy.

I, personally, felt the weight of the responsibility grow each year due the escalating calls we received from all over the country. We were the only facility around that would welcome and take care of distressed animals. I would share the glories and triumphs with the team but I tried to protect them from the stress and doubts.

We did not grow and expand through systematic planning but, instead, we grew as a reaction to the needs of the moments. Our growth was organic and natural in its manner. In less than two years we grew from caring for a few small animals like dogs, cats, sheep, and a turtle to; much larger animals with greater needs that were far more expensive to maintain. Not to mention the greater moral responsibility.

When we made the decision to open the facility to visitors I found myself in a place where I didn't like to be. I wasn't comfortable or eager to spend a lot of time talking and doing presentations. I'm not saying that to complain because with time I grew to love talking and educating people. As a former educator, I always enjoyed working with children but my experience in this matter was limited to working with them in the classroom.

The zoo gave me the opportunity to work with the children through a different way. By transmitting knowledge, I had the opportunity to pass something more important on to the children. Passion. The flame that was burning in my heart. My love of life. Life in all of its forms.

Using traditional teaching methods that one uses in a classroom environment did not work. I had a hard time capturing the attention and interest of the children. Here I discovered and learned that I had another talent which was to touch their hearts. Whether I spoke for ten minutes or an hour, children and adults would hang to my every word. I know that it wasn't due to my charm but rather the subject that I was talking about. The miracle of life. Their life. The respect of life. And the uniqueness of life.

What we were doing could only reach so far. My team and I could care for the animals at the shelter but our reach was limited beyond that. What we needed was an army to carry forward our vision. What I tried to do with the children was to inspire them to fight for life and to become the army that was going to make the real difference. They were, and are, our hope for the future.

Lots of people wanted to join our team. They wanted to work for us. But rare were the ones who stayed. Life at the zoo was challenging. The work was hard, the hours were long, but the hardest part was facing defeat and frustration. When you fight for life you don't win all the battles. I can even say that the number of defeats were greater than the number of successes. But, that is not a reason to abandon hope or the fight.

We had at the zoo more graves than cages. We buried more animals than we saved. That didn't take anything away from the value of existence, especially from the lives that we had succeeded in saving. The vulnerability of life doesn't take anything away from its value, but with the death of each animal someone on the team would leave. They took with them the spirit of celebration and they became our ambassadors wherever they went.

Rare were the ones who stayed and these were the pillars upon which the sanctuary grew. With them we kept saving more lives, decreasing the suffering of some, and offering a loving death of dignity for others.

The Team

The team of the zoo grew in parallel to the growth of the number of animals we had. We always had more work than the people to do it. The team was made from passionate people who never counted the hours. We used to start early in the morning until very late in the evening seven days a week. Every one of us came from a different professional background. What brought us together was the urgency to the cause.

Some of the team left their jobs or careers that they practiced all their lives and used to pay them well. Life calls to life. It was like falling in love and experiencing rebirth through the eyes of a loved one. They left everything without looking back and this was the same testimony that each and every one of the team members lived when they joined.

Joe was the welder whom we called every time we had to fix one of our cages. Usually he came for half an hour, maximum an hour, would do a job and leave. One day he had to spend an entire day to help us build a new cage. For the first time he had the opportunity to meet with the animals. At the end of the day he came to me and asked to have a place on our team.

Of course, I said no, thinking that this idea was coming from the excitement of the moment and that the next day he would change his mind. Joe had his business and was making a lot of money, much more than it could be possible to make form working with us. For six months Joe came every morning to ask me the same thing, "Could I join the team?" I had to say yes. Joe stayed by my side until the last day.

What to say about Reine and Tony? My most loyal companions and friends. Reine was here since the first step. She was a nurse who left her job as the nurse in charge of the emergency department of one of the biggest hospitals in Lebanon to join me in this adventure. And, again, until the last minute she was there by my side. In the hardest moments when the difficulties brought doubt to my heart she was there to confirm and reassure every one of the good foundation of our mission. Even today she is still ready to take up the torch and the dream again.

Tony, my dearest friend, one of the best zookeepers in the world. He's a war amputee. He lost his two legs to a mine. When I met him and since the first day, this man conquered me with his energy and his humor. The war took from him his legs but nothing from his passion and love. He used to be in the militia as a combatant and he adopted the cause of life and went to war against death.

Once, I asked him as a joke, "Tony with your amputation, how could you run if there was a risk of an animal attacking you?" He replied with a grin, "I'm the only one who doesn't have to run. I have nothing to fear. Worst for worst I would give him my wood leg."

To all these friends and companions and so many others that made this life possible I say thank you and we're not done yet.

What to say about the one who inspired me and supported me all the way through this adventure and so many others on the road of my life? The one with whom I shared every moment and every second. The one who when I lost everything, filled the emptiness with love and ignited to my life in the darkest moments. My sweet Katia, thank you for never abandoning or despairing. Thank you for all that love and loyalty. Thank you for believing in me and thank you for continuing to believe in me.

Chris and Jenny, my beloved kids, the youngest zookeepers in the world. Because of you I keep going.

I cannot forget the vital help a special man was providing to our animals. Every morning at 5 AM, he would go to all the grocery businesses to collect fruit and vegetables for our animals. And for me, every morning, he would bring a full load of love and affection, my dad.

I'm not offering all of this only as a tribute for all these people who made it happen, but to say that this project was not done by only one man. The efforts and the commitment of the people who got together and paid the price of the shared dream were what made it happen.

Crisis of Space and Money at the Zoo

As we grew and as we learned more, we ran into two major obstacles. We had no more space for new animals and the more we learned the more we discovered that the space we were offering them was not appropriate. All of the animals needed more room. We needed more people to take care of the animals which meant more money. Money that we didn't have.

We were able to be open to the public for four months of the year since the rest of the time it was either winter and cold or rain and dangerous. This limited our income from visitors. We needed more space and we needed more days that we could be open to the public. Because we had to look for a new location with a larger space it made sense to find a warmer location closer to the coast. We started to look and we found an amazing place by the river twenty minutes from downtown Beirut.

There was a restaurant built on the site and the owner was asking for fair market value. But, for us, fair market value was a lot of money that we did not have. At the same time, in addition to all of these problems we were having, the cold environment was beginning to affect the well-being of some of our animals.

Even after exploring all of the possibilities we couldn't see a way to do it. The site was perfect for all of our criteria but we just couldn't afford to do it.

A few days later I was having dinner at my cousin's place. I shared with him the situation and our troubles. He told me about a friend of his who was a big investor with a big heart. This friend might be interested and happy to invest in our operation. My cousin called him the same night and set up a meeting for the next day.

I went to the meeting and met my cousin's friend. He was a charming man who expressed his interest in our cause and expressed his willingness to help us with the expansion. He wanted to be a part of our project. He asked for a symbolic part of the zoo of 20% to just be a part of the family and to be sure that his money was going towards the well being of the animals.

Well, of course, I accepted. I wasn't a businessman and I didn't know a lot about business deals. I had no idea what a 20% stake would mean in the future. I was just excited by the idea of making this move possible and took him on faith alone.

I remember that we were in February. All the arrangements were taken care of. We got the property and it was like a dream place. There was a building at the front of the properly, what used to be the restaurant, and parking to the side of it. Behind the restaurant the property stretched out to the base of the mountains and was bounded by a river. The property was flat, open, and empty. It was like a paradise. In its former life it used to be a potato farm.

Before knowing that we were going to move I had made a layout for how the zoo would be at any new location that we would have. Of course, the design had some room for modification based on the form and shape of the land. The new partner wanted to consult with architects and engineers. In their opinion it was a two year project based on our plan.

My opinion was that from the moment we started building we would be operational in ninety days. Three months. We agreed with the new partner that if after the three months the zoo was not yet operating he would bring in his engineer to do the project.

This is how we started the new adventure.

It wouldn't be exaggerating if I said that I worked nineteen hours a day, seven days a week, for the full ninety days. Every evening I created the working plan of the next day. Every morning I made sure that everybody was executing the plan and following the schedule. On the 8th of May, 85 days from the day that we started, the zoo was ready to welcome the first visitors.

In the meantime, I got to know more and more of my new partner. Even with all his good manners I started to have doubts and fears. I began to suspect that there was more hidden to him than what he showed. And with different excuses he began to introduce new people to the team. These people were affecting the morale and the spirit of the project.

He began with his son. He introduced his son under the pretense that he wanted him to be in a protected environment so that we could watch over him. He introduced another guy who he said was a handyman and he owed him a favour so he needed to give him a job. He introduced his accountant who he already paid a salary to so we wouldn't need to pay him ourselves.

I said yes to all of these people because I didn't see any reason not to and I wanted to help him out.

What started to cause me doubts and fear about my business partner's intention was that he only showed excitement over the potential revenue. He never asked a question about the animals and he didn't seem interested about learning more. But, every time that I had a doubt, he would do something to alleviate it leaving me with a guilty feeling for feeling that doubt. For example, he would invite me over to dinner and we'd have a great time.

I ended up finding excuses for his behaviour. I would say to myself things like, maybe I'm not used to having a business partner. As an investor, of course, he is interested to see his money grow. You need money to make money. You need revenue to cover the expenses of the project.

During this period, I was focused on the deadline and the construction. Physically and emotionally I was very tired. These were very long days and they were exhausting. Our first serious disagreement happened two weeks before the grand opening.

It was about the entrance fee.

He wanted to bring the fee up to $10 from the $2 that we had. For me, I saw the importance of getting more money to cover our growing expenses. My solution was to grow the number of visitors and have more opening days. That would generate more money but that would keep the mission and the spirit of the project which was to be an educational project and a sanctuary for the animals.

For my partner, he had a plan in which there were three years to make the maximum money out of this project before it died. After three years people would, in his mind, lose interest in the zoo. This was contrary to the spirit and vision of the project. The idea was to keep offering a safe place for animals and a continuous educational program for people.

Because he had all the arguments regarding what we may be facing as expenses I agreed to the $10 entrance fee even though I wasn't happy with it. He said it was better to start with a high fee and lower it later instead of starting with a low one and raising it. And he was right; we had far more expenses to cover, so we needed the income to cover our operational costs.

Moving from the Zoo to an Apartment

One of the hardest consequences of moving to the new location was for me and my family. We couldn't live on the premises of the zoo anymore. There wasn't any appropriate accommodations for us there. We rented an apartment about thirty minutes away from the new zoo and up the mountain. Living away from the animals in a building apartment was a huge change. Our extended family was no longer around.

Although the distance wasn't huge we still felt that we lost something. A big part of how we lived was no longer there. We had a new life, a new rhythm to adapt to. It was sad but the thought that all of these changes were going to be for the best interest of the animals gave us the strength to adapt. This new location for the zoo had incredible potential and we hoped that we would one day be able to move back to the zoo, our home.

More Crocodiles

With our new location and greater visibility to the public we received an ever increasing number of calls from people with animals in need. We had a call from a guy who owned or managed a kind of beach resort where they would host animal shows. He asked if we could meet because he had an urgent matter regarding animals to discuss with me.

When we got there he took me to a large indoor amphitheater that had a large pool. In this pool were three large crocodiles. He told me how they had hosted a crocodile show but there was a money disagreement at the end of the show with the group. He kept the crocodiles and the organizer left the country without taking them.

A significant problem presented itself to him. He was hosting a dolphin show immediately after the crocodile show. The dolphins were supposed to live in the pool that these three large crocodiles were currently occupying. All that he wanted was to get rid of the crocodiles because the next day the dolphins would be arriving. He wanted us to take them or to shoot them. Of course, our choice was clear but there was a simple problem, we had never captured crocodiles. I had never even seen a live one this big.

I had always been fascinated by the Crocodile Hunter series with Steve Irwin. The part of the series that always amazed me was how he would catch crocodiles. I had memorized all of the techniques and methods he used imagining that one day I would do it. I didn't really believe that this day would actually come in my lifetime. Yet, here I was standing in front of the crocodiles not only imagining how I would do it but also imagining what would happen if something went wrong. One word was repeating in my head, "Crazy, Crazy, Crazy."

I went back to the zoo and I asked two of our zookeepers to come with me. We got a rope, duck tape, and we went back to the resort. It took us about two hours of debating to decide how we were going to immobilize the crocodiles and catch them. I ended the discussion by deciding to use the method I had seen on television. This was to jump on the back of a crocodile and wrap my arms around the mouth to clamp it shut.

Our final plan wound up being this: one of the zoo keepers would grab hold of the crocodile's tail immediately after I jumped on the back and clamped shut its mouth. The second zookeeper would quickly wrap a rope around the jaws and then duct tape the crocodile's feet to the crocodile's body to completely immobilize it without hurting it.

We gave the owner a stick and told him to keep the other crocodiles away in case they attacked us. You might wonder why we didn't call someone with a tranquilizer gun. There was a problem with that on that day. In the whole country there was only one person that we knew who owned a tranquilizer gun and it was our vet. On that day he was out of the country and it was impossible to reach him. We only had that one day to save the lives of these crocodiles.

With my heart pounding in my chest I jumped on the first crocodile's back and everything went just as we planned. The first zookeeper lay with all of his weight on the tail and the other one was very fast with rolling the rope around the mouth and then taping up the feet. The whole operation for the first crocodile took less than five minutes.

The other crocodiles did not move while we did this. The success of the first operation gave us courage and we thought how easy it was to catch a crocodile. We shifted our attention to the second crocodile to do the same thing. This one gave us some resistance but the operation went great. We managed to subdue the crocodile without any real difficulties.

The third crocodile started to move around. We decided to wait about an hour for two reasons. The first was that we wanted the crocodile to calm down and the other reason was that our muscles were spent. Wrestling crocodiles with adrenaline pumping turned out to be strenuous exercise. The third and final crocodile was the biggest of the three. We had decided to leave it for last so we could practice on the other two.

After recuperating some strength and seeing that the largest crocodile had settled I did the same maneuver and I jumped on the crocodile's back and clamped his jaws shut.

This time, however, when I had hold of his jaw the crocodile kept moving. The zoo keepers were shouting because the crocodile had thrown the one at the back off its tail. Being free the crocodile flipped onto its back pinning me beneath it. I was being crushed and suffocated by this crocodile and then it flipped again. I took this moment to let go and roll off the other way escaping the angry crocodile.

The crocodile had its mouth tied but the legs were free and it was moving in the water. It was impossible to get to it because we were exhausted and hurting. We were scared now to do the same thing again. We decided to get a huge cover, much like a tarpaulin, and we caught the crocodile on top of it. We lowered the tarp into the water and maneuvered it beneath the crocodile then we rolled it up with the cover and tied it.

This is how we managed to bring three crocodiles to the zoo. Thinking about it now I think that we were crazy but we managed to save the lives of these three crocodiles with our craziness.

# Hyena

At the new zoo we had learned from our experiences in how we constructed our enclosures. We designed them with double doors and strong fencing. Each animal was given as much space as we could and they had the shade they needed. We had a temporary holding enclosure where the door was designed differently. The temporary holding cage had its door in two parts. An upper part and lower part each of which could be opened independently.

We designed this cage door so that it would open up away from the cage. To get in, we would pull it open and not push it open like the other cages. This was the only door we did this with and we did it this way so that we could have a carrying box on the ground sitting at the door. With the door being opened away from the cage it was on hand for the keepers. We could open the lower cage door, place the box, open the box, pull the box out and shut the door very quickly.

Once a hunter brought us a wounded hyena. We called the vet he took care of the injuries. Before the hyena woke from the anesthesia we took advantage of the few minutes that we had before it would wake up to transfer the hyena into a large carrying box. Our idea was to put this box in the temporary holding cage and leave it there. This way the hyena would wake up in a protected shelter inside the holding cage.

I was going to go into the cage, open the box, and run out. There would be someone at the door who would open the door for me and then close it immediately once I was out. There was practically no risk because the hyena was under the anesthesia. hen we got the box to the cage we found out that there wasn't enough shade in the cage for the hyena. We left the hyena in the box and quickly gathered materials to create the shade. It took us about half an hour to create the shade structure and because of this the hyena was fully awake in the box when we were done.

This meant that I would have very little time, maybe two seconds, to open the box and then escape the temporary holding cage as the hyena emerged. Because the hyena was under anesthesia and was going to be in the temporary cage for about a week we had put the box at the far end of the cage from the door. The cage was about twenty feet in length and that was the distance I would have to travel before the hyena came out of the box. We guessed that the hyena would be mad upon waking up so I would have to move very fast.

I went into the cage and opened the door of the box. I ran towards the cage door shouting at the worker at the door to open it. Once I got to the door and started pushing something happened to cause the worker to panic. He pushed the door shut locking me into the cage.

What made him panic was something he saw but I didn't. I looked behind me and saw the hyena coming out of the box. At that moment, not knowing what to do, the worker kept pushing the door closed. The more I pushed the more he did. Caught in the moment, the worker was only thinking of the loose hyena, and I was trapped inside the cage.

I took a deep breath and asked him to listen to me and just let go. He released his hold and I escaped from the cage. Hyenas aren't normally aggressive animals and they don't attack humans but we didn't know much about hyenas at the time. For me, I was just locked in a cage with a savage and angry hyena. What made me panic at that time makes me laugh today since I wasn't really in as much danger as we thought I was in.

We didn't know much about most of the animals when they arrived. We never used our lack of knowledge as a reason not to rescue an animal. Our first motivation was to save lives. I think this is what kept us going even if, at some times, we were taking stupid risks.

Charley Continued

The whole time with the zoo, I kept contacting organizations that take animals in captivity and release them into the wild. Some of our animals, our guests, would never make it in the wild because of their injuries or handicaps. But, many of our animals would do great in the wild and would live happier and more productive lives in their natural environment.

The most qualified of our animals for this was Charley the chimpanzee. Charley was a very smart chimpanzee and the main thing about him was that he was very affectionate. Even though he was very social we could tell that there was a shadow of sadness in his eyes. Charley needed a home with other chimpanzees.

I had this dream for Charley to find him a great home where he could belong and live free. I kept searching for possibilities and came across a website for the Pan African Sanctuary Alliance (PASA). I contacted PASA with an email and they responded. We sent back a few emails and I invited them to come and visit the zoo. Surprisingly, they accepted the invitation and came for a visit.

During this process I kept my partner informed about what was happening assuming he was on board since he started with our mission of protecting the wellbeing of our animals and putting whomever is able back into their natural habitat. He never showed much enthusiasm about this part of our mission but he never argued or expressed disappointment.

I always believe that despite all our disagreements about profitability these weren't major as long as we shared the same value regarding the future of the animals. There were many times that I felt a discomfort and thought that I saw red flags but I kept hoping that I was going to get him to adopt the view that we have for the zoo. That we were using the term zoo as only a practical public identification to get people to visit our mission was still to protect and educate. Everything we did should fall under that mission.

I kept putting all of his questionable suggestions and maneuvers as business behaviour. I never had a doubt that he might have a plan to take over the project and turn it to a pure profit business. Some of my team members who had more close contact with the people that he introduced to the zoo tried to warn me that something wrong was going on. That this guy had bad intentions. I never wanted to listen to this kind of gossip.

At the same time, the daily work and the worries were taking priority so I didn't give it much thought. I really regret this today.

We finally got the visit from PASA. My team and I were really excited. This was the first time we got the attention of an international organization. Even if everybody was sad to the idea of losing Charley we pictured him jumping, playing, and being free with a newfound mate in the jungle. We had an amazing meeting with the representative of PASA. We made arrangements for the transportation and move of Charley.

We needed about a month to raise the money, do some fundraising, and make all the arrangements with vets and authorities so that Charley could be transported to his new home. The next day, I had a meeting with my partner to inform him of the good news. At this meeting I saw an expression on his face that I had never seen before. He went crazy.

He kept repeating the same sentence, "Do you know how much money we are going to lose by losing Charley?" I tried to convince him using his own arguments by explaining how much publicity we would get from doing this. This was true because PASA was ready to invest money in a public awareness campaign about our sanctuary and about the illegal trade of animals. This would bring us international exposure.

The only thing my partner saw was the loss of the money by letting Charley go.

We ended the meeting with opposite views and I couldn't convince him. I realized that it was never going to be the same and that he had never adopted our mission. I knew that he would never allow Charley to go. I had a long fight to set Charley free. What I didn't know, at that time, was how well connected my partner was politically.

The next day, my partner visited the zoo. He was very nice like we never had the conversation the day before. He didn't mention it and didn't say anything about Charley. The only thing he spoke to me about was that he needed to offer a job to a young girl that needed two months of work for her tuition. He wanted her to be at the front entrance selling tickets. I had no issues with that and I wanted to rebuild the trust between us so I said yes.

He called the girl and she came and started working that same day. He came back that evening told me that his accountant was creating a new system where he needed to collect, every day, the money from the ticket sales. He told me that there would be no issues with our operational costs. Any time the zoo needed anything he would give me a check.

Two days later I arrived to the zoo and began my regular inspection round. I felt something strange, something different. Every time I stepped into the zoo I could recognize the sound of every animal from far away. That day I knew that something was missing. Something was wrong. I couldn't figure out what until the moment I reached Charley's cage.

The cage was empty.

I wasn't very worried at that moment because sometimes I knew that the workers at the zoo let Charley free for a while before the gates opened. I had forbidden them to do this but knowing how Charley can be insistent occasionally they would disobey me to placate him.

I used the walkie-talkie to call the zookeeper on duty and asked him about Charley.

He told me that he hadn't gotten to his cage yet but Charley was supposed to be there. This was when we began the search. Charley was nowhere in the zoo. It was impossible that he would escape or run away. Any time Charley was free he would either follow the zookeeper or he would go to where he knows where the food is. He wasn't there and none of the zookeepers had seen him.

We spent the day looking for Charley, wondering where he could be. Stealing him was not an option because it was impossible to get inside the zoo without breaking in. There was no sign of breaking in. In the evening, my partner passed by to collect the money. When I told him about Charley he asked me to stop thinking about it. When I asked what he meant, he said just know that Charley is in a safe place.

At that time I understood that my partner was willing to do anything to not let Charley go. I thought that if I threatened to leave the zoo that would scare him because he had no idea on how to take care of the animals. So, I told him that if Charley did not come back I would leave.

He looked at me, smiled, and said, "Please, be my guest. That would be your choice."

From that moment, we were unable to get from him a dime of the money collected. We started getting short on food for the animals. We got to the end of the month with salaries to pay and we had nothing in the accounts. Every time I asked him for money his answer was, "Why do you need money? You don't care about money. Find a way to feed your animals to pay your salaries. We have more important bills to pay."

I started using our own money, really my wife's money, to buy the food for the animals. I didn't have a salary from the zoo yet. That was going to start in another couple of months from this time. It was part of my agreement with my partner to give the zoo as many resources as possible to grow and expand.

I used to drive from my house to the zoo every morning at around 6 AM. The road was quiet, narrow, and very curvy. The road went down the mountain and many of the curves were very sharp. I would drive very slowly, like 20 kilometers per hour, as I planned my day. This way I didn't have to focus so much on the road and would let my mind think about the day. This was the only quiet time of the day that I had before facing the daily challenges.

I remember that day I was really sad. A feeling that I wasn't familiar with. The zoo used to bring me so much joy and contentment. I used to live at the rhythm of the zoo now I was living at the rhythm of the problems. We lost the farm in the excitement.

I used to start the day with an attitude of welcoming whatever that day would offer. Now, I started my days wondering and fearing what this day would strike me with. It wasn't a life I wanted to live. It wasn't what I wanted to fight for or to invest my life in. I was very deep into my thoughts when I felt that something was going wrong with the car.

The whole car was shaking and it was taking me to the side of the road. To the cliff . . . Because I wasn't able to steer it back I braked. I succeeded in stopping it before the edge of the cliff. I stepped out of the car, I checked on the tires, and I saw that the passenger's front tire was tilted. I called a mechanic that I knew and he came with his tow truck.

When he lifted the car, the tire fell off. This was when the mechanic discovered that all six of the bolts that hold the tire in place were cut. He said they had been cut with a saw. This was something he had never seen in his entire career. He'd had customers with one broken nut but never all six of them.

On the road to the zoo and about two minutes from the zoo there was a small house by the woods. It was an abandoned house and I had gotten to know the owner who had a gas station where we filled all of our vehicles. Later that same day, I asked the guy if there was any possibility to get the house for a good price. He offered it to me for free as long as he had no tenants and, in exchange, we would do all the repairs that the house needed.

I transformed it into an office where I started meeting, every day, with my original team to figure out how to face what was happening. How to understand what was happening and how to come up with a plan to face what was happening. Things were becoming serious and out of control. The animals were hungry, some were almost starving, they weren't getting the care that they needed, and some of the workers were leaving.

We knew my partner was paying his own people at the zoo. In the meanwhile, the PASA people who had left Lebanon were counting on me to send them our part of the plan for Charley. I had avoided telling them what was happening while I tried to gain time and regain Charley. They started getting more insistent because their part of the plan was getting ready. They had found a place for Charley, they had made the contacts, and they were just waiting for the green light from us. That they could come and make it happen.

I had so many stormy discussions with my partner. I don't want to go into the details. Every time he kept repeating, "If you want to provide your animals, your team and their family with what they need, let me take over."

The situation put me in despair. I didn't have any more money neither to feed the animals or my own family. The problem escalated so much that the only solution that I could see possible was to leave the zoo.

My partner was offering to buy me out. I don't know how to explain what was going on inside of me. It was a mixture of regrets that I brought this person in, disappointment, anger, and a lot of sadness. I was sad to death at that moment this guy was already taking over.

He had already taken over. I knew it and so did he. The only solution to keep this project alive was for me to go away.

Now that I think about it, I know that there were so many other solutions and possibilities I could have pursued. It's easy now to say that I should have fought, I could have done something. That leaving wasn't an option. But, at that time, I was overwhelmed, young, and had never faced so much aggressiveness and such a calculating person.

I left the zoo.

A New Life

Every morning I would go to the abandoned house in the woods near the zoo. I worked on fixing up the house and every afternoon the core members of my old team would come and visit. They kept asking me what my plan was. I had none.

They were expecting me to do something, ro come up with a plan, a solution, a path forward. But I was lost and unable to think in a practical way. I had lost. I felt that I had lost everything: my animals, my dreams, my project, my team, and my self-confidence.

A week later, Tony, Reine, Joe, and the other team members came as usual after their shift and told me that they were all fired, they were being replaced by new people. That was catastrophic especially for the animals. Who was going to take care of them? The new people didn't have a clue on what to do. They didn't have any experience, any expertise, and definitely no passion.

With no jobs and no income we kept meeting every day to try and figure out a solution to save the animals. For two weeks we talked, we debated, and we struggled to find something. In the end we came up with nothing. The fate of the zoo was out of our hands.

How could this be possible?

I could not accept defeat. With my team looking to me, my family looking to me, the animals looking to me, I started coming up with crazy ideas. I thought about breaking into the zoo and setting the animals free. I thought about protesting; but, I knew that none of these ideas were practical nor would they help the animals or us. Those weren't solutions.

My team and I were going through true hell. The zoo had been our home. The animals were our family. How could we abandon them?

My partner had been preparing his move long time before I figured out what was happening. While we were taking care of the project, he had kept himself busy destroying our image and reputation. So when we tried to call some common friends in the hopes of assistance and help they wouldn't give it to us. They were against us or, at best, they didn't want to be taking sides.

It was a lost cause at this point, it had already been a month and I couldn't protect the animals. I had to face the consequences of my decisions and what had happened.

I had lost the zoo.

I had lost the zoo but my team was still together. They didn't want to leave me. They had families to feed, bills to pay, all the reasons in the world to leave and go on their way but they were fighters. They believed in the cause, they were fighting for and this could not be the end.

We created a new dream, a goal, and a plan. We wanted to create a sanctuary, a place to promote life and to educate people on how to protect life. We wanted to build a civilisation of life. We would have to start from nothing. All what we had was that dream and the will to make it happen. But, we had done it before with the zoo.

The dream was still alive and its fire was hotter. The will was stronger then ever. The moment we realised that we had the possibility to turn another dream into reality, a new door was opened. A new great adventure had begun.

The loss of the zoo wasn't the end but the beginning of a new journey, Dino city.